READ-TOGETHER TREASURY

BIBLE STORIES

publications international, ltd.

A NOTE ABOUT THIS READ-TOGETHER TREASURY

This is a special book. It is designed and written to be shared between an experienced reader and a beginning reader, taking turns reading aloud.

The treasury is extra-wide so that it can be easily spread across two laps. The experienced reader — Mom or Dad, Grandma or Grandpa, even an older brother or sister — sits on the left and reads aloud the left-hand pages. These pages are written using the classic storybook prose that children love to hear, but may not yet be able to read on their own.

The beginning reader sits on the right and reads aloud the right-hand pages. These pages are written especially for early readers. The type is larger and less intimidating, the vocabulary is basic, and the sentences are short and simple.

This book provides the perfect opportunity for a young reader to hone his or her reading and comprehension skills. The positive experience of reading together with a loved one will encourage a love of reading in children. And the quality time spent as you take turns reading may be the greatest reward of all.

Please enjoy this unique book, full of stories to read aloud, stories to treasure…stories to share.

My child, listen to me and treasure my instructions.
Tune your ears to wisdom,
and concentrate on understanding.
–Proverbs 2:1-2

TABLE OF CONTENTS

Adam & Eve

Retold by Lynne Suesse
Illustrated by Karen Pritchett

God created everything on earth. He took his time. Every flower and tree was unique. Every animal was special. He drew each tiger stripe and painted every butterfly wing with care. Monkeys could swing from the mighty trees. Birds could sing songs to each other as the sun rose in the morning. God was satisfied with all that he created on earth. He looked at all the creatures, from the tiniest insect to the greatest elephant, and he was pleased. But he was not finished. God wanted to create something extraordinary.

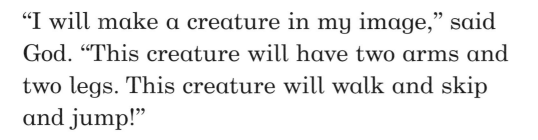

"I will make a creature in my image," said God. "This creature will have two arms and two legs. This creature will walk and skip and jump!"

God made the dust on earth move. The dust rose and swirled. Then the dust settled. God looked at the new creature he had made.

God named the creature Adam, which means "man." Then Adam named all the other plants and animals on earth.

God wanted to make a place for Adam to live. He thought Adam's home should be the loveliest place on earth, so God created a garden in Eden. In the garden, he planted the prettiest flowers and trees with the most delicious fruits and seeds. In the center of the garden, God planted the tree of knowledge of good and evil. But God felt that man would be lonely with only plants and animals for company.

God told Adam to go to sleep. While Adam was sleeping, God took a rib from Adam and made a second creature in his image. God looked at this new creature. He called it woman, which means "of man."

When Adam woke up, he saw woman. He was very happy. She was the prettiest creature that he had ever seen. God told Adam she was made from his rib.

Adam took woman's hand and said, "You are a part of me. We are one. I will call you Eve because you are the mother of all living things. Eve means 'life.'"

God showed Adam and Eve the garden.

"This is where you will live," God told them.
"It is your home. Enjoy the animals. Eat the
fruits and seeds from the trees."

Adam picked two juicy peaches from a nearby
tree. He took a big bite from one of the peaches.
He liked it very much.

God said, "You may eat from any tree
except one. Do not eat from the tree
of knowledge of good and evil."

God showed Adam and Eve the tree.
They agreed to obey God's wishes.

God smiled at Adam and Eve. Then he left them alone in the garden.

Adam and Eve loved the beautiful garden that God made for them. Eve put flowers in her hair, but she did not mind that she did not have clothes. Adam did not mind that he did not have clothes either. Adam and Eve did not know what clothing was. They were not embarrassed about showing their bodies. All they knew was that they loved their home in the garden.

One day, Eve took a walk to see and smell her favorite flowers. She loved all the flowers in the garden, but her very favorite flowers grew under a large tree. She liked to sit under that tree.

When she looked up from where she was sitting, Eve saw an unusual snake. The snake began to talk to her. The snake asked her all kinds of questions about the garden.

"What do you eat?" the snake asked.

"Adam and I can eat whatever fruit we want," Eve told the snake.

"What about fruit from this tree?" the snake asked.

"God told us not
to eat this fruit,"
said Eve.

"Really?" asked the
snake. "Why?"

"God told us not to eat this fruit,"
Eve said again.

Eve told the snake that bad things would happen if she ate the fruit.

"Is that what God told you?" asked the snake. "God knows this fruit will open your eyes. That is not a bad thing."

"God told us not to eat this fruit," Eve said.

Eve looked at the fruit on the tree of knowledge of good and evil. She looked at the fruit for a long time.

She wondered if what the snake said was true. If she and Adam ate the fruit, nothing bad would happen to them, but the fruit would open their eyes. Adam and Eve would be able to see everything. They would know as much as God!

Looking closer at the fruit, Eve thought it looked good to eat. She called to Adam and told him about the snake. She told him that if they ate the fruit, they would be rewarded. The fruit would open their eyes.

Eve quickly plucked a piece of fruit from the tree of knowledge of good and evil. She took a bite of the fruit. It tasted delicious.

"Does it taste bitter?" asked Adam.

"It's wonderful," said Eve.

Adam did not hesitate after that. He grabbed the fruit from Eve and took a bite. He could not believe that God would keep them from eating such wonderful fruit.

Then something strange happened!

Adam felt like he could see better. Eve felt like she could see better.

Adam and Eve could see the garden better. The garden looked different.

Adam and Eve could also see they were not wearing any clothes. Eve hid behind a bush. Adam grabbed some leaves.

Soon Adam and Eve heard the voice of God. They were afraid. They hid from God, but he quickly found them. God was very angry with them for hiding from him.

"Why are you hiding from me?" asked God.

"We are hiding because we are naked," said Adam.

"How do you know that you are naked?" asked God.

Adam told God that Eve picked the fruit from the tree of knowledge of good and evil. Adam said they both ate the fruit that God told them not to eat. Adam explained that after eating the fruit from the tree of knowledge of good and evil, they felt ashamed to be without clothes.

God asked Eve if this were true. God asked Eve if she had picked the fruit and eaten it.

Eve told God how she had been tricked by a snake. She told God how the snake said the fruit would open her eyes. God searched the garden for the snake and cursed the snake.

Then God gave Adam and Eve clothes made of animal skins. When they were dressed, he told them to leave the garden.

God was still very angry with Adam and Eve. He told them that they could never come back into the garden.

"The garden is no longer your home," said God.

Fruit and nuts did not grow outside of the garden. Adam and Eve had to grow their own food. They worked hard, and the new plants grew.

God still loved Adam and Eve.

Noah

Retold by Alison Pohn

Illustrated by Mike Jaroszko

There once lived a good man named Noah. He lived thousands of years ago when the earth was new.

But almost all of the people on the new earth had become wicked. They did not know right from wrong. They were not kind or caring. They were not hardworking. They did not respect and love God.

God was disappointed in the people. He decided to flood the earth and let all the people be swept away. That is, all the people except for Noah, his wife, their three sons, Shem, Ham, and Japheth, and their wives.

God went to Noah and told him to build an enormous boat, called an ark. The ark would keep Noah and his family safe during the flood.

Noah lived in the desert. He had never built a boat before.

So God told Noah exactly how to build the ark.

God told Noah which wood to use.

God told Noah where to put all the windows and doors.

God told Noah how tall to make it.

God told Noah how wide to make it.

God told Noah how long to make it.

Then Noah built the ark.

Noah worked and worked, and finally the finished ark stood in the middle of the desert. It was enormous!

The ark was way too big for Noah and his wife and his sons and their wives. That was because they were not going to be the only passengers on the ark.

God had thought about what would happen after the flood, and he wanted to make sure that the world would be filled with all the animals and birds and insects that were already in the world. God told Noah to gather all the animals of the earth. He told Noah to place on the ark seven of every kind of animal and bird that people eat and two of every other kind of animal and bird and insect.

Noah also needed to bring along food for all of those animals and birds and insects. He also needed to bring food for his family.

That was why the ark had to be big!

Soon the ground shook. The air was filled with noise. All the animals, birds, and insects came to the ark.

They walked toward the ark in happy pairs.

There were eagles and elephants and earthworms.

There were skunks and swans and squirrels.

There were buffaloes and bats and butterflies.

Noah and his family helped all the animals get safely into the ark. Then they waited.

For six days they listened for the pitter-patter and splish-splash of rain, but no rain came. The ark stood, dry and still on the desert sand.

Finally on the seventh day they heard something, but it was not the sound they had expected. It was not the pitter-patter of a gentle rain. It was not the splish-splash of a few raindrops. It was the roar of the heavens opening up and a deluge of water coming down upon the earth.

Noah and his family watched as the rain soaked into the sandy earth. Then the ark slowly lifted off the ground. Noah and his family and the animals felt the ark begin to rock. They realized they were floating higher and higher as the water rose and rose.

First the water covered the ground. Soon the water covered the trees. Then the water covered even the tallest mountains. All Noah and his family could see was water and rain and more water. Outside the ark, they could see that the whole earth was flooded.

But inside the ark, it was very safe. Noah and his family, the animals, the birds, and the insects were snug and dry and warm.

The horses were calm. The doves were still. The lions were peaceful. The dogs did not bark. The cats did not scratch.

Noah, his wife, their sons, and their wives took care of all the animals. They knew just what to do for each animal.

The horses liked to eat oats. The doves liked to eat bread crumbs. The lions liked to be scratched. The dogs liked to be petted. The cats liked to sleep.

The rain did not stop. Noah and his family never even saw the sun peek through the clouds. Noah was worried that the ark might leak, but not even a drop of water got in.

For forty long days and forty long nights the rain continued. Then on the forty-first day Noah heard a strange sound. It was the sound of quiet.

There was no rain banging on the roof. There was no wind howling through the windows. There was only the sound of a gentle breeze and the occasional sound of an animal or bird or insect.

Noah opened one of the windows of the ark and looked out upon the world. There was still water for as far as he could see. He went to the other side of the ark and saw the same thing.

Every day for one hundred and fifty days, Noah looked out the windows of the ark and saw only water. But the next day, Noah felt a sudden strong wind. It blew hard over the water.

Then the ark stopped rocking, and everything was still.

Noah did not know if there was any dry land.

Noah sent a raven into the air to find dry land, but the raven came back. She could not find dry land.

Noah waited. He waited some more. He waited six days.

Then on the seventh day, he sent a dove into the air to find dry land. This time the dove came back with a leaf in her beak.

Everyone cheered.

There was dry land!

Noah wanted to make sure his wife and sons and their wives and all the animals and birds and insects would be safe, so he had everyone stay inside of the ark for seven more days.

The animals pawed at the floor of the ark, the birds flew around in the air, and the insects crawled and flew. They were all ready to leave the ark.

Finally on the eighth day, Noah threw open the doors to the ark. He stepped outside the ark for the first time in over two hundred days. It felt strange not to see any water. It felt strange to be on dry land.

The first thing Noah did was thank God for bringing him and his family and all the animals and birds and insects to safe, dry land. God told Noah it was safe for him and his family to leave the ark. He told Noah it was safe to let the animals and the birds and the insects go out into the world and fill it with more animals and birds and insects.

Then God made a promise. He promised he would never again flood the earth. As a sign of that promise, God created the rainbow. The rainbow arched across the sky.

Then the ground shook. The air was filled with noise. All the animals, birds, and insects came out of the ark.

They walked out of the ark in happy pairs.

There were eagles and elephants and earthworms.

There were skunks and swans and squirrels.

There were buffaloes and bats and butterflies.

Joseph

Retold by Alison Pohn

Illustrated by Jon Goodell

In the land of Canaan, there lived a man named Jacob who was the father of many sons. The sons were named Reuben, Simeon, Levi, Napthali, Isaachar, Asher, Ephraim, Zebulon, Manasseh, Gad, Benjamin, Judah, Dan, and Joseph.

Joseph was happy because he knew God was with him. He was good and hardworking. The same could not be said for his brothers.

Joseph was his father's favorite son. All the brothers knew this, and they did not like it. The brothers were jealous of Joseph.

Jacob even gave Joseph a very special coat. It had every color imaginable. The coat made the brothers even more jealous of Joseph. Why should Joseph get such a coat, and they get nothing?

The coat had more colors than the rainbow.

It had the blue of the brightest sky, the green of the growing grass, the white of the wooly lamb, the purple of the pretty flowers, and the red of the rising sun.

Joseph loved wearing his coat. He almost never took it off.

He wore it in the morning. He wore it in the fields when he was watching the sheep. He wore it at night. Sometimes he even wore it when he went to sleep.

Joseph worked hard all day, and at night he slept and he dreamed.

In one of Joseph's dreams he and his brothers were working in the fields. They were tying wheat into bundles. That was not so unusual. But then a very odd thing happened in the dream. The wheat bundles started to move by themselves. Then Joseph's bundle of wheat stood up. Slowly, each of his brothers' bundles of wheat stood and bowed down to Joseph's bundle.

Joseph told his brothers about this strange dream. The dream made them angry.

"My bundle bowed to Joseph's bundle?" said Asher.

"Joseph's bundle should bow to mine," said Zebulon.

The next night, Joseph had an even stranger dream. He saw the sky, and in the sky he could see the moon and the stars shining upon him. The moon and the stars moved toward Joseph. Then the moon and the stars bowed down to him.

After hearing this dream, Joseph's brothers got mad again.

"What is this dream you have dreamed?" asked Jacob.

Joseph told his father about the dream.

"Is everyone supposed to bow to you?" asked Jacob.

Joseph did not want to explain the dream.

Jacob was upset with his favorite son, so he sent him to tend the sheep in the far field with his brothers.

Joseph put on his colorful coat and went out to the far field like his father told him to do.

But long before Joseph spotted his brothers, his brothers saw him coming because they could see his coat.

"I've had it with him," said Isaachar.

"He thinks he's so special in his fancy coat," said Levi.

The brothers put their heads together and came up with an evil plan. They would throw him into a pit and say a wild beast had eaten him.

Reuben, the oldest brother, knew that this was wrong, but he was afraid to stand up to his brothers. Reuben planned to secretly come back and rescue Joseph when his brothers were not around.

"Joseph!" called Asher. "Come over here and look what fell into this pit."

When Joseph got close to the pit they grabbed him. They tore off his beloved coat and threw him into the pit.

Joseph was not scared. He knew that God was with him.

From far away, the brothers saw some merchants coming toward them.

"I have an idea," said Gad. "Let's sell Joseph to the merchants. They'll take him far away. Good-bye to father's favorite!"

"We'll tear the coat and give it to Father. He'll think a beast ate Joseph," said Dan.

So the brothers sold Joseph to the merchants as a slave.

When Joseph's brothers told their father their lie and showed him Joseph's torn coat, Jacob wept and wept. He had lost his favorite son and could not be consoled.

The merchants took Joseph to Egypt, but Joseph was not scared because he knew God was with him. The merchants sold him to a man named Potiphar. Joseph worked hard for Potiphar, and Potiphar noticed what a hardworking and trustworthy man Joseph was. He made Joseph the head of his whole staff and trusted him to run his house. But Potiphar's wife was like Joseph's brothers. She was jealous of Joseph. She got Joseph in trouble with Potiphar by lying.

Joseph was put in prison. In prison, he became friends with another prisoner, a man who had worked for the Pharaoh as a servant.

"I've had the strangest dream," said the man.

"Tell me what you dreamed," said Joseph.

"I dreamed of three branches," said the man. "The branches burst into buds. The buds burst into grapes. I gave the grapes to the Pharaoh."

"The dream means you will return to work for Pharaoh," said Joseph. And the man did!

When Pharaoh started having strange dreams, the servant took Pharaoh to see Joseph in prison.

Pharaoh told Joseph his dreams.

"Seven healthy cows were eaten by seven sickly cows. Then seven good ears of corn were eaten by seven rotten ears of corn," said Pharaoh.

"Can you tell me what these dreams mean?" asked Pharaoh.

"They mean that Egypt will have seven years of good crops," said Joseph. "Then there will be seven years of famine."

"What should I do?" asked Pharaoh.

"You must put someone in charge of storing food during the first seven years," said Joseph. "Then there will be enough food during the next seven years to keep everyone fed."

So Pharaoh freed Joseph and gave him that job.

During the first seven years, Joseph made sure that abundant food was stored. Then the famine arrived, and families came from miles around to share the saved food.

Joseph recognized his brothers when they came, but they did not recognize him. Joseph remembered how they had treated him, but he hoped they had changed.

He decided to test them. He hid a silver cup in Benjamin's pack. When Benjamin was caught with the cup, Joseph had him thrown in prison, but each brother tried to take the blame to save Benjamin!

It was then that Joseph knew his brothers had changed.

"Look!" said Joseph. "It is me, your brother Joseph!"

The brothers were sorry for what they had done to him.

They were happy to see Joseph. They bowed down to him, like the stars in the sky had bowed in the dream from so long ago.

When Jacob saw Joseph, he also bowed to him like the moon had in the dream. Jacob wept with joy to see that his favorite son was alive!

Miriam & Moses

Retold by Lynne Suesse

Illustrated by Kathy Mitchell

Miriam and her mother lived in Egypt. Miriam's mother was pregnant with a new brother or sister for her.

They had a happy life like many other Hebrew families, but life in Egypt began to

change. Egypt had a new king. This new king, called Pharaoh, did not like the Hebrew families. He felt threatened by the fact that the Hebrews in Egypt had such big, happy families. Pharaoh thought that someday the Hebrew families would outnumber the Egyptian families.

So Pharaoh tried to make life tough for the Hebrews. He made them slaves, but the Hebrew families only grew stronger.

When Miriam went to the market for her mother, she met a woman. The woman was a friend of the family.

"Good morning," said Miriam.

The woman did not smile. She was very sad.

"What is wrong?" asked Miriam.

The woman told Miriam that the new king had a terrible plan. He wanted every newborn Hebrew boy to be drowned in the river.

Miriam turned and ran home as quickly as she could.

Miriam ran and ran. As soon as she saw her mother, she began to cry.

"What's the matter, my sweet child?" asked Miriam's mother.

Miriam told her mother what the woman at the market had said about Pharaoh. She told her that she was afraid for the new baby.

Miriam's mother was frightened, but she did not want Miriam to know that she was afraid. She sent Miriam out to play. Then she asked her neighbors if what Miriam had told her was true. They said they had heard the same stories.

The next day, Miriam's mother gave birth to a new baby. It was a boy! Miriam and her mother were so happy they cried for joy. But they also cried many tears of sorrow. They were afraid that Pharaoh's men would come to take the baby from their home.

"What will happen to my new brother?" asked Miriam.

Miriam's mother did not know. She did not want Miriam to be afraid.

"He will be fine," she said, "but do not tell our friends that your brother has been born."

Miriam's mother told her that the baby was a secret. Miriam and her mother kept the baby a secret for three months.

But as the baby grew bigger, he was hard to hide.

For three long months Miriam and her mother hid the new baby inside the house. They had to discourage any visitors, so Miriam would tell the neighbors that her mother was not feeling well. All that time, Miriam's mother sat with her new baby and worried that someone would find out the truth. She did not want to lose her new son.

Then Miriam's mother had an idea.

"If Pharaoh wants the river to have my son, then I shall give my son to the river," she said.

Miriam's mother told her to collect as many large bulrushes as she could find. Miriam knew that the largest and strongest stalks of bulrushes grew near the river's edge. She went there to gather as many as she could carry.

When she returned home with the bulrush stalks, Miriam and her mother wove them into a tiny boat for the baby. The boat would float on the river, and the baby would not drown.

Soon, the little boat was finished.

Miriam was very proud at how sturdy it was.
She knew that her brother would be safe.

The next day, Miriam's mother told Miriam
to take the baby to the river. She told
Miriam to put the baby and the boat
into the water. Miriam did what
her mother asked.

But Miriam could not leave
her brother alone in the water.
She sat on the river bank. She
hoped someone with a kind
heart would find him.

Soon Miriam heard some voices. Some people were coming! Miriam quickly hid in the tall river grass. She left her brother, safely tucked into his homemade boat.

Miriam peeked at the approaching strangers. She saw a beautiful woman who looked like a princess. The woman was accompanied by two young girls. All three of them were dressed in rich clothes.

Miriam heard the woman ask one of the girls to fetch her a drink from the river. As the girl walked down the bank, she spied the tiny boat. As she got closer, she saw that the boat had a baby inside.

"Bring him to me," said the woman as she held out her arms to the baby. "I will keep this child for my very own."

The woman was the daughter of Pharaoh. She realized that the baby boy was a Hebrew.

"I will call you Moses," said the woman. "It means, 'from the water.'"

Miriam heard the women talking about the baby.

She heard the woman say the baby needed a nurse. The nurse would help to raise the baby. The nurse would keep the baby away from Pharaoh.

When Miriam heard this, she stepped out of the grass. She told the woman that she knew a Hebrew woman who would like to raise a baby.

The woman agreed to let Miriam take the baby Moses to his new nurse.

Miriam held her brother close and went home as quickly as she could. She could not wait to tell her mother of their good fortune.

She could not wait to tell her mother that Pharaoh's daughter found the baby. Above all, she could not wait to tell her mother that she would be able to take care of the baby!

When Miriam's mother saw her son, she could not believe her eyes. She did not understand why Miriam had the baby with her.

Miriam explained what had happened at the river's edge. Miriam's mother was so happy, she hugged and kissed her daughter. Then she held her precious son and cried for joy. When Miriam left with the baby in the little boat, Miriam's mother did not think she would ever see her son again.

Soon Moses was no longer a baby. He was a little boy. He liked to play games with Miriam. He liked to hear the stories his mother told to him.

But Moses knew he had to go live in the palace soon.

One day, Moses went as close to the palace as he dared. He saw the king. He wondered if the king would like him.

Moses did not know what life in the palace would be like. He did not yet know he would lead his people, the Hebrews, to Israel.

Ruth & Naomi

Retold by Lora Kalkman

Illustrated by Marty Noble

When a famine struck Israel, Elimelech and his wife, Naomi, took their two sons to Moab. There, the sons married young Moab women. Then sadly, Elimelech and both of his sons passed away. This made Naomi very sad.

"Go home to your mothers," Naomi said to her daughters-in-law. "I will go back to Bethlehem in Israel."

"I will miss you," said Orpah. She left Naomi and Ruth.

"I could never leave you all alone," Ruth said.

"You should go back to your family," Naomi said.

"My place is with you," Ruth said.

Ruth and Naomi went to Bethlehem together.

They arrived just in time for the harvest.

Ruth saw that Naomi was hungry.

"I will go to the fields," Ruth said.

"You must be careful," Naomi said.

"I will be careful," Ruth said.

Naomi kissed Ruth good-bye.

Ruth kissed Naomi good-bye. Then she walked to the barley fields.

During the harvest, many people worked picking the barley. Then the barley was ground into flour that was used to make cereal and bread.

Ruth approached the man in charge, called the foreman.

"Dear sir," she said, "I am Ruth, Naomi's daughter-in-law. We have just come to Bethlehem from Moab, and we have nothing to eat. May I help to harvest the barley? Then, perhaps, you would let me keep some to eat."

"Since you are part of Naomi's family, you are welcome here," the foreman said.

Later that day, the owner of the fields came by.

The field owner was a good man named Boaz, and he was related to Naomi's husband, Elimelech. They were family.

"Who is that young woman over there?" Boaz asked his foreman, pointing to Ruth.

"She is Naomi's daughter-in-law," the foreman said.

"What is her name?" Boaz asked.

"Her name is Ruth," said the foreman.

"Why is she picking barley?" Boaz asked.

"She has no food," the foreman said. "She asked to help. She is a hard worker."

Boaz went to Ruth.

"You are part of my family now," Boaz said. "You will work in my fields. You will not be hungry. I will protect you."

"But what have I done to deserve such favor?" Ruth asked Boaz. "I am just a foreigner here, and you are so kind."

"I have been told what a hard worker you are," Boaz said. "It must have been hard for you to leave your own family and move to a foreign land. Naomi was all alone, but you stayed by her side. You are a very kind woman. May the Lord repay you for what you have done."

"Thank you," Ruth said.

"You shall have dinner with us," Boaz said.

When it was time for dinner, Ruth sat down with the other harvesters. She had a hearty meal of roasted grain and bread, which she dipped in wine vinegar. When she was full, Ruth tucked away some leftovers for her mother-in-law. Then she returned to the fields where she worked until evening with the other women.

That night, Naomi was awaiting Ruth's return.

"How was your day?" Naomi asked.

"It was a good day," Ruth said. "I met a man named Boaz. He said I could work in his fields."

"Boaz is related to my husband," Naomi said.

"I did not know that," Ruth said.

"He is a good man," Naomi said.

"He said he would protect me," Ruth said.

"May God bless Boaz for his kindness," Naomi said.

Ruth continued to work in the fields and to look after Naomi.

During the day, she joined Boaz's workers in the barley fields. After they had finished harvesting the barley, they began to harvest the wheat.

When they were thirsty, they fetched cold, clear water from the well. They always ate their meals together.

Ruth enjoyed the company of these women. She made many good friends and looked forward to each day.

But Ruth also missed Naomi during the day. In the evenings, she rushed home to Naomi. Ever thoughtful, Ruth always brought food for her.

"You are such a kind girl," Naomi told Ruth.

"Thank you," Ruth said.

"You should have a family of your own," Naomi said. "Then you would have a child of your own someday to look after you."

"I would love to have a husband and a child," Ruth said.

"Boaz would make a fine husband," Naomi explained. "He is good and kind."

Ruth washed. She put perfume on her neck. Then she went to see Boaz.

Boaz was working. He was making grain into flour. He looked up when he saw Ruth. He smiled.

"Hello," Boaz said.

"Hello," Ruth said. "I came to help."

Ruth handed some grain to Boaz.

"I also came to talk to you about something," Ruth said.

Ruth told Boaz that she wanted to be his wife.

Boaz also longed to get married and have a child.

"Let us get married," Boaz said.

Boaz told everyone in Bethlehem that he planned to marry Ruth. The townspeople were very excited. A lovely wedding was held, and everyone attended.

As a gift, the couple received new land. It was the land once owned by Elimelech, Naomi's husband.

"You have earned this land," Naomi told Ruth. "You have been very good to me. You are my daughter."

On the land, Ruth and Boaz built a new home and planted more crops. Ruth was very happy. She still saw Naomi every day and often invited her to dinner. Then one evening, Ruth had joyous news.

"I'm going to have a baby," Ruth said.

Several months later, Ruth gave birth to a son. Ruth named the baby Obed.

Obed was a happy baby.

Obed made his mother very happy.

Obed made his father very happy.

Obed made Naomi very happy.

Naomi loved to hold Obed in her lap. She loved to hug him. She loved to kiss him. She loved to rock him. She loved to sing to him. She loved him very much.

"Dear God," Naomi said. "When I was alone, you gave me Ruth. Now you have given me Obed. Thank you, Lord, for giving me a family again."

Samson

Retold by Leslie Lindecker

Illustrated by Cheryl Roberts

The Israelites were conquered by the Philistines after forty long years of fighting.

Manoah and his wife lived in Israel. They were sad because they had no children. They prayed that God would bless them with a child.

One day, God sent an angel to Manoah's wife.

"Behold, you will soon have a son," the angel said. "Do not cut his hair or shave his head. He will serve God from the time he is born. He will grow up and save Israel from the Philistines."

Manoah's wife hurried to tell him what the angel had said. Manoah was not sure he believed it.

He prayed to God, "Lord, please send the angel to teach us what to do."

God listened to Manoah. He sent the angel back to talk to Manoah and his wife.

"Are you the angel who spoke to my wife?" asked Manoah.

"I am," said the angel. "Everything I said will happen soon."

Manoah and his wife rejoiced.

When their son was born, they named him Samson.

Samson grew up strong. God blessed him. Samson loved God and he loved his mother and father.

When Samson was a grown man, he met a young Philistine woman. He told his parents that he wanted to marry her.

Samson went to visit the young woman. Along the way, a lion attacked him. God gave him strength. Samson killed the lion with his bare hands, but he did not tell anyone what had happened.

When Samson made another trip to the young woman's house, for the wedding feast, he passed the body of the lion he had killed. Bees had built a hive in the body of the lion. It was rich with honey. Samson took handfuls of honey to the feast.

Many young Philistine men came to Samson's wedding feast. They wanted to trick Samson because he was an Israelite.

But Samson could be tricky, too.

"Let me tell you a riddle," Samson said to the Philistine men. "If you solve it in seven days, I will give you gifts. If you cannot solve the riddle, you must give me gifts."

Samson told the men his riddle. "Out of the eater came something good to eat," he said. "Out of the strong came something very sweet."

The young Philistine men could not solve the riddle.

"Find out the answer for us!" they said to Samson's new wife.

She went to Samson. Samson told her about the lion. She ran back and told the young Philistine men.

The young men found Samson and told him they had solved his riddle.

Angry that he could not trust his new wife, Samson returned to his father's house without her. Then Samson forgave his new wife. He went to see her father, but her father would not let Samson in.

"I thought you would not come back," her father said. "I gave her to a man who was your friend. Her younger sister is more beautiful than she is. Perhaps you would want to marry her instead."

Samson became angry again. He caught three hundred foxes. He tied torches to their bushy tails. He lit the torches and set the foxes free to run among the crops of the Philistines.

The Philistines saw all their crops burning.

"Who has done this terrible thing? Everything is burning!" they cried.

"Samson did this," someone said. "His father-in-law gave his new wife away to his friend."

The Philistine men went to find Samson. They were angry with Samson.

Even some Israelites were angry with Samson for what he had done.

"The Philistines are looking for you," they said.
"We will tie you up and give you to them."

"Promise you will not hurt me," said Samson.

The Israelite men promised.

Samson let them tie up his hands and
his feet.

The men took Samson to the Philistines.

The Philistines shouted when they saw
Samson. They were angry with him.

When the men gave Samson to the Philistines, the spirit of the Lord came over Samson. The ropes that tied him fell away from his hands and feet.

Samson found the jawbone of a donkey and struck down the Philistine men who wanted to hurt him.

Samson asked God to help him. God split a rock and water came out of it. Samson drank the water. He was refreshed. He praised God for helping him.

After that, Samson went from place to place. Stories of his great strength went before him. The Philistines wanted to capture him, but they did not know how.

One day Samson met a beautiful woman named Delilah. He fell in love with her.

"Trick him," the Philistines said to Delilah. "Find out where his great strength comes from. We will give you a great fortune for this information."

Delilah went to Samson.

"Please tell me why you are so strong," said Delilah. "Is there nothing that can bind you?"

"Tie me with new ropes," Samson said.

But the new ropes broke away as soon as Samson was tied.

"If you love me, you will not lie to me anymore," said Delilah.

Samson loved Delilah. He could not lie to her.

"If my hair is cut," said Samson, "I will lose all my strength."

When Samson was asleep, Delilah had a man cut off Samson's hair. As soon as Samson awoke, the Philistines arrested him.

Samson was bound with shackles and chains. The Philistines put him to work in the prison. It was hard work for a man of regular strength.

But Samson's hair continued to grow.

The Philistines celebrated because they had captured their enemy. A party was planned. When the people gathered, they called for Samson to be brought to them to amuse them while they ate.

Samson was led from the prison to entertain the people gathered for the celebration. Samson spoke to the boy leading him.

"Let me lean against the pillars of the house," Samson said.

The young boy led Samson to the center pillars of the house.

With all the Philistines watching, Samson placed one hand on one pillar and one hand on the other pillar. Then he prayed.

"Lord God," said Samson, "please strengthen me once more."

Samson pressed one pillar with one hand. He pressed another pillar with the other hand.

God answered Samson's prayers. God gave Samson strength.

The pillars of the house gave way.

The house fell on Samson and all the Philistines in it.

Samson had freed Israel from the rule of the Philistines.

David & Goliath

Retold by Kate Hannigan

Illustrated by Douglas Klauba

"Fill your horn with oil," God said to Samuel. "I am sending you to Bethlehem to anoint the next king."

Samuel obeyed God's command. Samuel was a prophet, and God revealed to him certain things that were to happen in the future. In Bethlehem, Samuel would meet a man named Jesse.

Samuel found Jesse and asked to meet his sons. Jesse told each son to step forward. The eldest, Eliab, approached first.

"He is strong and handsome," Samuel thought. "He will be the next king of Israel."

"People see the outside," God said, "but the Lord looks on the heart."

Samuel met seven of Jesse's sons.

God told Samuel that none of these sons was the next king.

"Are there more sons?" asked Samuel.

"David is in the field," said Jesse. "He watches over the sheep."

"Bring him to me," Samuel said.

"This is David," God told Samuel. "He is the one. Open your horn of oil and anoint him."

"The spirit of God will be with you always," the prophet said to David.

At this time, the king of Israel was an old man named Saul. Saul disobeyed God, and an evil spirit came upon Saul and made him feel bad.

"I'll find someone who is a good harp player," said his servant. "When the evil spirit is upon you, the music will make you feel better."

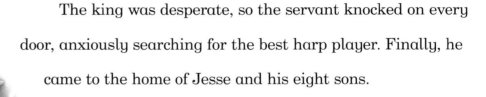

The king was desperate, so the servant knocked on every door, anxiously searching for the best harp player. Finally, he came to the home of Jesse and his eight sons.

"My boy David plays the harp like an angel," Jesse said.

"May I take him to the king?" asked the servant.

Jesse agreed and sent David with the servant. David played for the king, and when Saul heard the beautiful music that came from the harp, he began to feel better.

"That is the most glorious sound," whispered the king.

Saul asked David to visit often. David did and played his harp for the king. The evil spirit left Saul for good.

David was a very good harp player.
He played all of the time.

He played for the king. He played
for his family. He even played for
the animals.

"What do you think, little sheep?" asked
David. "Do you like this music?"

The lambs came close to David. They loved to
hear him play his harp.

David was a very good harp player. He made the king very happy.

"You are a blessing to me," said the king.

David proved himself a worthy musician, but he was also a strong fighter. Not only could he play the harp like an angel, he could use a slingshot like a soldier.

One day as he tended his flock on the hillside, a lioness crept into the field. She skulked through the brush, hungrily eyeing the sheep.

David walked among the sheep, unaware of the dangerous lioness. As he was walking, he stooped to pick up a tree branch and saw a flash out of the corner of his eye.

Swoosh! David looked up just in time to see the lioness pounce on a lamb, snatching it up in its teeth.

The tiny lamb let out a cry. In an instant, David reached down and grabbed a stone the size of his fist. He slipped the stone into his sling.

"Let go of the lamb!" shouted David as he leapt onto a boulder. "I'll slay you! I am not afraid!"

The lioness held down the little lamb and let out a mighty roar.

David swung his sling faster and faster. Around and around it went.

David let the stone go. It flew through the air.

It was like a shot. It hit the lioness in the head.

The lioness roared in pain. David grabbed the lamb.

"Take this!" David cried as he flung another stone.

The stone hit the lioness. The lioness fell. David defeated the lioness and saved the lamb.

After David's battle with the lioness, another battle was taking shape in the valley. King Saul and his men gathered on one side. Their enemies, the Philistines, gathered on the other side.

The Philistines were led by a fearsome fighter called Goliath. He was frightening to behold. He wore a helmet of brass, thick chain mail on his chest, and wide armor on his legs. His spear was so long and so heavy, no other man could carry it.

"What are you afraid of?" Goliath shouted. "Send down a man brave enough to fight me. If he beats me, then my people will be your servants. But if I beat him, then you will be our slaves!"

Saul and his men listened to Goliath and trembled. He was the scariest soldier they had ever faced. For forty days Goliath taunted them, and they were more frightened with each passing day.

And with each passing day, Saul's soldiers grew more and more hungry. Jesse sent David to bring them food.

David brought the men bread and cheese. They ate, but they were not very happy.

"Why is everyone afraid?" David asked. "Goliath is just a man."

David's brother became angry. He told David to go back to the sheep.

"I will fight Goliath," David said.

"But you are just a boy," said the king. "Goliath is a man of war!"

"I beat a lioness," David said. "I can beat Goliath."

David was confident, and he told King Saul he would not be defeated.

"God delivered me safely from the lioness," said David. "He will deliver me from this terrible man."

Saul tried to protect David. He tried to dress him for battle in thick armor, a coat of chain mail, and a heavy brass helmet. But David would not wear them. He shook everything off.

David reached down and picked up five stones for his sling.

As David approached the giant, Goliath let out a loud laugh and mocked the boy and his sling.

"You come to me with a spear and javelin," David said, "but I come to you in the name of the Lord!"

Before the giant could raise his spear, David dropped a stone into his sling and began to swing it. In one quick flash, he let it fly.

The stone hit Goliath squarely between the eyes.

Goliath fell.

Just as he beat the lioness, David beat Goliath. David won!

"You did it, David!" shouted Saul and his army.

People were proud of David. They sang songs about him.

Many years later, King Saul died. People remembered David's courage. They put a crown on his head. They made David king of Israel.

It was just as God told the prophet Samuel it would be.

Esther

Retold by Kate Hannigan

Illustrated by Sally Schaedler

Long ago in the days of King Ahasuerus, there lived a young woman named Esther. Esther had lost her parents, so her loving uncle, Mordecai, raised her as his own.

Esther was smart and beautiful, and she had a good heart. She was kind to everyone she met, from the bakers to the shepherds to the servants of the king. She was so kind that when the king met Esther, he fell deeply in love.

"I will hold a feast for Esther," said the king.

At the feast, the king declared Esther his queen. He was very much in love with her.

The king threw a party for Esther. Everyone had fun.

Uncle Mordecai had fun, too. Then he heard two men talking.

Mordecai listened. The men wanted to hurt the king.

"The king must be warned," Mordecai thought.

Mordecai ran to tell Esther what he heard. Esther told the king. The king punished the bad men.

"Mordecai," said the king, "you saved my life."

The king had many advisers to help him govern his vast kingdom. His top adviser was a man named Haman, who loved the feeling of power.

"People should bow down before me!" Haman thought.

Many people did bow before Haman, but Mordecai, who was Jewish, refused to bow to him. Mordecai would not worship false idols. This made Haman angry, and he plotted to hurt Mordecai.

"Mordecai and his people will be punished," he said.

Haman went to the king with a plan. He told the king that there were certain people in the kingdom who would not follow the laws.

"We must destroy them," Haman urged.

The king agreed. He gave Haman his ring, which bore the official seal of the kingdom, and every province was told about the plan to attack the Jews on the specific day Haman had chosen.

Mordecai heard about Haman's plan. He was sad.

He went to tell Esther.

"The king must do something to help our people," Mordecai said.

Esther was Jewish. She had never told the king. Now her life was in danger. All the Jews were going to be destroyed.

"I will go to the king, myself," Esther said. "I will ask him to help us."

"Be careful," said Mordecai. "Haman is an evil man. Watch out for him."

It was dangerous to ask the king for favors. He was powerful and did not want to be bothered with trivial things. If he did not like what he heard, the king could deliver a harsh punishment.

Still, people traveled from all corners of the kingdom for a chance to speak with him. They filled the courtyard, waiting patiently for days and days.

Esther paced nervously among the crowd in the courtyard, knowing it was dangerous to ask anything of the king. She was risking her life. But when the king saw her standing among the rest of the people, he called her to him.

"What is it, my beloved Esther?" he asked.

Esther was afraid, but she had a plan. Her hands trembled as she knelt before the king.

"I am hosting a banquet tonight," she said. "I would like you and your adviser Haman to attend."

"Haman and I would be pleased to attend," said the king.

The king went to Esther's party. Haman went to Esther's party. They ate good food. They listened to music.

"What do you want, dear Esther?" asked the king.

Esther was afraid to speak. She was too nervous.

"Come again tomorrow night," Esther said. "I will tell you then."

The king was happy. Haman was happy. They liked parties. They said they would come again the next night.

After Esther's party, the king met with his advisers to discuss business. He wanted to know how Mordecai had been rewarded for saving his life. His advisers told him Mordecai had not been rewarded.

"We must reward Mordecai!" the king shouted. "Call in my chief adviser!"

Haman was summoned to the king's office.

"What shall we do to reward the man who helped me?" asked the king.

Haman smiled a wicked smile and stroked his beard. In his arrogance, Haman thought the king wanted to reward him.

"He should be dressed in the finest robes and led through town on a beautiful horse," said Haman.

"Good plan," said the king. "Now hurry with fine robes and a sturdy horse to carry Mordecai through town. Tell everyone how he helped the king."

Haman was furious.

"This is an insult!" thought Haman. "I must get rid of Mordecai as soon as possible."

That night, Esther had another party.

"What is your wish, dear Esther?" asked the king.

"Someone wants to hurt my people," she said. "I need your help."

"Who is trying to hurt your people?" asked the king.

"That wicked man!" said Esther.

She jumped up and pointed at Haman.

"I am Jewish," said Esther. "Haman wants to hurt all the Jewish people."

The king banished Haman.

Haman left the kingdom, and the king promoted Mordecai. He gave him Haman's job.

But there still was work to be done. Risking punishment again, Esther asked another favor of the king.

"Haman has sent soldiers to hurt my people," she said. "Let me warn my people so they can defend themselves."

The king granted Esther's request. He gave her his ring with the royal seal.

Esther and Mordecai had to act fast. They sent riders to every province, telling the Jewish people to rise up and defend themselves.

The king's messengers rode as fast as they could to deliver the news. They were able to warn the Jews just in time.

Esther's people waged a fierce battle, defeating Haman's soldiers. Instead of a day of massacre, it was a day of great triumph for the Jews.

Esther was brave. She had courage. She saved her people.

Her people were happy. They celebrated. They marked the day on the calendar. They called the special day Purim.

Every year, they celebrated Esther's courage. They told their children about it. Their children told their own children.

To this day, the Jewish people still remember Esther's great courage. They celebrate Purim every year.

Jonah & the Whale

Retold by Virginia R. Biles

Illustrated by Tom Newsom

Have you ever thought about not minding your parents? Of course not! You know that your parents would be very upset with you, and they would probably punish you for disobeying. This story is about a man who tried to disobey God.

Jonah was a good man who lived in the country of Israel. The people of Israel worshiped God and believed they were God's people. Israel had been at war with the neighboring country of Assyria for many years. Nineveh was the capital of Assyria. Nineveh had stood for hundreds of years, and thousands of people lived there. The people of Israel did not like the people of Nineveh. When Jonah thought about the horrible city, he prayed to God to destroy it.

"Defend your people against their enemies," Jonah prayed. "Destroy our enemies."

The people of Nineveh did not know about God.

The people of Nineveh worshiped idols.

Some idols were like people. Some idols were like animals. Some idols were like people with animal heads.

The people of Nineveh were selfish and wicked.

"I will destroy all the people of Nineveh," God said.

But God decided to give the people of Nineveh a chance before he destroyed them.

God decided to send a prophet to Nineveh. The prophet would tell the people there about God.

One day, Jonah was walking by the sea when he heard a voice speaking to him. It sounded deep like thunder, and Jonah knew it was God.

"Jonah," said God.

"Yes, God," said Jonah.

"I want you to go to Nineveh, Jonah," said God. "Tell the people there that I am angry that they are worshiping idols. They must either change their sinful ways and follow me or I will destroy them and their city."

Jonah loved God, but he hated the people of Nineveh. He wanted God to destroy them. He certainly did not want to save them from God's anger.

He thought and thought about what he could do to keep from going to Nineveh. He walked up and down the shore. Then he came up with a plan.

"I will not go to Nineveh," Jonah said to himself. "I will go far away. God will not be able to find me."

Jonah went to a seaport. He looked at all the ships. Finally, he found one that was going far away. It was going to a city named Tarshish.

"God will not be able to find me there," Jonah said.

Jonah paid his fare and went aboard. The sailors raised the anchor. The wind blew on the sails. The ship left the seaport.

Jonah felt safe.

Jonah was very tired after trying to escape from God, so he went down into the hold of the ship. He spread a mat on the floor and fell asleep.

God knew, however, where Jonah was. He knew that Jonah was disobeying him. He was angry with Jonah, just like your parents would be angry if you disobeyed them.

As Jonah slept, the skies grew dark. The winds began to blow harder. The waves grew larger and larger. As the wind howled, the sails began to rip. The ship struggled. The sailors were frightened.

"What have we done to cause this storm?" they asked. They prayed to their gods, but the harsh wind became harsher. The waves grew larger.

Finally the captain of the ship went to Jonah, who was still sleeping peacefully below deck.

"Wake up!" he shouted. "Pray to your god to save our lives!"

Jonah knew that God was causing the storm. He knew that God would not listen to his prayers because he had tried to run away.

Jonah went up on deck.

Jonah knew he was the cause of the trouble. He knew God was angry with him.

"Throw me overboard," Jonah said, "and God will save you."

The sailors did not want to throw Jonah overboard. They did not want to die either.

"May your god be with you," the captain said.

The sailors threw Jonah over the side of the ship.

The water was cold, and Jonah fought to keep his head above the waves. The saltwater made him cough, and it stung his eyes.

He watched the ship grow smaller and smaller, until he could no longer see it.

Yet, he did not pray to God to save him. Just as he was sinking beneath the water, a whale swam up from the depths of the sea. It circled Jonah. Then it opened its large mouth.

Jonah felt himself being picked up. Then he slid into darkness. He was inside the belly of the whale.

Jonah was cold, but he could breathe. Every time the huge whale swallowed, cold water rushed in.

Jonah knew he would die inside of the whale.

After three days and three nights, Jonah wanted to tell God how sorry he was for disobeying.

"Lord," Jonah said. "I put my wishes before your command. I was afraid. Please forgive me."

God heard Jonah's prayer.

Jonah felt himself move forward. There was a great rush of water. The whale spit him out on the shore. Then the whale swam away.

Before Jonah could get to his feet, he heard a deep voice. He knew it was God's voice.

God was not finished with Jonah. Jonah knew that.

"Jonah!" said God. "You must go to Nineveh!"

"Yes, Lord," said Jonah. "I will go."

Jonah went to Nineveh. The people looked at him and wondered who he was. Jonah spoke loudly so everyone could hear him.

"The Lord is angry with you," Jonah said. "If you do not stop worshiping false idols, God will destroy your city!"

Jonah had done what God told him to do. He did not think the people of Nineveh believed what he said. He hoped God would destroy them all, but God had other plans.

The people of Nineveh believed Jonah when he said that God would destroy them if they did not change their ways. They changed. They tore down their idols. They took off their fancy clothes and put on sackcloth. They stopped eating rich foods, and they fasted. They prayed to God and promised to be good people.

Jonah went out to the hillside and waited for God to kill the people of Nineveh. He was unhappy, but God caused a lovely plant to grow over Jonah's head. It shaded Jonah, and he was at least pleased with that.

The next day, God caused the lovely plant to die.

Jonah began to cry. He was very sorry the beautiful plant had died.

Then Jonah heard the voice of God again.

"Jonah," said God. "Why are you crying for the plant? It is not a person. You should care about the people of Nineveh. I have saved them just as I have saved you."

Jonah knew that God was right.

God was always right.

Amen.